Cognitive Behavioral Therapy

How to Overcome Phobias, Addictions, Depression, Anxiety, and Other Problematic Disorders

By Lance Pettiford

I0412897

Table of Contents

Introduction

Cognitive behavioral therapy has been around in its modern form since the 1970s. Since it was first developed, it has been tested again and again in countless clinical trials and experiments. The most effective parts were kept and those that were found to be less effective were abandoned or replaced with better ones. All this has resulted in the emergence of one of the most promising and rigorously tested therapeutic techniques ever to exist.

Today cognitive behavioral therapy involves a highly efficient system for targeting your problems, treating them at the source, and developing skills you will need to prevent that problem from occurring again. And the best part of it all is that you can do this all on your own. You don't have to pay for expensive therapy sessions or attend outrageously priced therapeutic retreats. You can simply pick up a book (like this one) and learn about the strategies and techniques involved and begin treating yourself today!

There are countless proven techniques used in cognitive behavioral therapy methods that have been specifically designed to treat the most urgent problems many of us face in our lives. While cognitive behavioral therapy has been shown to be effective in the treatment of countless disorders, this book will focus on treatment techniques for the four disorders that cognitive behavioral therapy has been the most effective in treating. Those four disorders are phobias, addictions, depression, and anxiety disorders.

With this book, you have access to a comprehensive guide to using cognitive behavioral therapy methods on yourself. In the following chapters you will learn more about:

- Exactly what cognitive behavioral therapy is, how it was developed, and what the general process involves.

- The specific techniques that cognitive behavioral therapy uses to treat the four disorders mentioned above, including: cognitive processing therapy, exposure therapy, acceptance and commitment therapy (ACT), cognitive therapy, relaxation training, and dialectical behavior therapy.

- The cognitive distortions that are involved in the negative thought processes and how to identify them.

- A guide to conducting your own mental health assessment so that you can better understand exactly what is wrong and what needs to be fixed.

- A guide to cognitive behavioral therapy treatments for phobias.

- A guide to cognitive behavioral therapy treatments for addiction.

- A guide to cognitive behavioral therapy treatments for depression.

- A guide to cognitive behavioral therapy treatments for anxiety disorders.

- Extra tips for those who plan to use cognitive behavioral therapy methods entirely on their own (that is, without any additional support from a professional).

- Warning signs and indicators that your problem may be too severe to treat on your own (in other words, how to tell when it is time to seek out the help of a professional), and;

- Additional resources that can help you treat yourself using the cognitive behavioral methods described in this book, including free online cognitive behavioral therapy courses and programs.

So keep reading and learn how you can use cognitive behavioral therapy to improve your life!

Chapter 1: An Overview of Cognitive Behavioral Therapy

Cognitive behavioral therapy came about as a combination of the behavior therapy techniques developed by Donald Meichenbaum and the cognitive therapy techniques developed by Albert Ellis. It is a therapeutic approach used to treat a wide variety of emotional dysfunctions or unbeneficial behaviors. The major characteristic that distinguishes cognitive behavioral therapy from other therapeutic approaches is that it is much more systematic and goal oriented.

So, while psychoanalysis is more open ended and used to probe into a person's mind; cognitive behavioral therapy uses specific, practical techniques to change the unwanted thought process or behavior. One advantage of being so systematic is that you do not necessarily need a therapist to successfully use the techniques of cognitive behavioral therapy.

A therapist can, of course, be helpful as a guide or source of motivation when things get tough but, in general, you can successfully treat yourself with the techniques described by cognitive behavioral therapy. In fact, even if you do have a therapist, a large part of the work will be done by you since you have to apply the strategies to your everyday life. This contrasts with psychoanalysis, for example, where the therapist does the bulk of the work because it is their job to do the interpretation and analysis.

This therapeutic approach has had the most success in treating depression and anxiety disorders. In fact, it has been shown to be just as effective as antidepressant medications (and with cognitive behavioral therapy, you do not have to worry about any of the side effects that you have to with medication). In addition to depression and anxiety disorders, cognitive behavioral therapy has also been used successfully to treat other mood disorders, personality disorders, eating disorders, addiction, phobias, and even psychotic disorders.

The reason that cognitive behavioral therapy is so effective in the treatment of so many disorders is because it is so problem oriented. This approach operates on the understanding that negative or harmful thought processes are the primary factor contributing to negative or harmful behaviors and emotions. Therefore, cognitive behavioral therapy targets those thoughts processes. There are two general strategies used to deal with these negative or harmful thought processes.

The first strategy is changing the thought process itself. This involves various techniques (depending on the specific problem at issue) for identifying, isolating, and eliminating a negative thought. Usually, in this process, you also work to cultivate positive thoughts that are meant to take the place of the original negative ones.

The second strategy involves changing your relationship to the negative thought process (rather than changing the thought process itself). This requires you to constantly challenge these negative patterns of thinking or beliefs and thinking consciously about them. That means understanding what sort of errors in thinking (or cognitive distortions, as they are called in cognitive behavioral therapy) are involved. For example, perhaps you are running a slight fever and your first thought is that you have some form of untreatable cancer. Rather than eliminating the thought and replacing it with a positive one (as you would with the first strategy), you instead examine the thought and realize that it is an example of magnifying negatives and catastrophizing (two types of cognitive distortions which you will learn more about in chapter 2).

By understanding exactly how a negative thought is flawed (beyond the simple fact that it is negative), you can take the power from it and no longer allow it to control your behavior or your emotional state. This will also help you to tell the difference between rational negative thoughts (such as genuine signs of serious illness) and the irrational ones.

Both of these general strategies are highly effective ways of treating serious problems. In this book, you will learn self treatment methods that combine both so that you can not only strip a negative thought of its power but replace it with more positive ones.

Within these two general strategies, there are a variety of specific methods used which includes exposure therapy, cognitive processing therapy, acceptance and commitment therapy (ACT), dialectical behavioral therapy, and relaxation training. All of these have their own specific methodology but each has the same ultimate goal of greater self-awareness. You will learn more about them in chapter 2 (as well in later chapters which deal with the treatments for specific problems).

We can break the cognitive behavioral therapy process down into six generalized phases:

1. Mental health assessment: this is an important preliminary step in which you simply work to identify exactly what your problem is. Are you depressed? Are you anxious? Are you suffering from a phobia or addiction? Assessing your current mental and emotional state will already bring you one step closer to achieving full self awareness. You will begin with this phase of the process in chapter 3.

2. Reconceptualization: this phase is more based on the "cognitive" side of cognitive behavioral therapy. It is in this phase that you begin identifying and challenging the negative thought processes which are causing the problem (or problems) you identified in the first phase.

   Reconceptualization involves both understanding the cognitive distortions at work (discussed in chapter 2) and replacing these negative thoughts with positive ones. The specific techniques for doing this depend on your specific problem. You will learn more about the techniques you can use for reconceptualization in chapters 4 through 7.

3. Skills acquisition: in this phase, you begin the process of learning the new coping skills you will use to both overcome the current problem and get through troubling situations in the future without falling back into the same negative behaviors you are used to. These coping skills can be either cognitive or behavioral skills and will depend largely upon the specific problem you are dealing with. You will learn about the specific coping skills for phobias, addiction, depression, and anxiety disorders in chapters 4 through 7.

4. Skills consolidation and application training: in this phase, you put together a plan using the specific coping skills you have learned and want to use in your cognitive behavioral therapy treatment. Then, you start practicing the skills according to the plan you have created. This is typically the most intensive and time consuming phase because you are essentially retraining your brain and trying to develop new habits.

5. Generalization and maintenance: by this phase, you will be more or less used to the new coping skills you have been working on throughout phases 3 and 4. Now, all you need to do is make them a part of your daily routine and use them in all challenges that you face rather than just those relating to the specific problem you were treating.

6. Post treatment assessment and follow up: if you have been working with a therapist,

this is something that you will do with them. Otherwise, you can essentially do another mental health assessment to see what progress you have made and what areas you may still be struggling with. This may seem like an unnecessary step but it is actually very important. By doing a post treatment assessment, you can take the time to appreciate how far you have come. You can also see what problems you might still be struggling with and go through these 6 phases again to treat those.

All in all, the duration of these six phases and the whole cognitive behavioral therapy process in general will depend on the severity of the problem. However, in most cases you will begin to see positive signs of change in your thought process and behavior in as little as 6 weeks. And after about 6 months, you will notice much more dramatic results. Typically, if you work at it consistently, by the end of the 6 months, the positive skills you have been working on will have become more or less habits (meaning you will be around phase 5 or 6 of the process).

Because the ultimate goal of cognitive behavioral therapy is to achieve greater self awareness, you will actually continue to use these techniques long after your problem has been treated. This is because cognitive behavioral therapy is not so much a one-time treatment as it is a method for changing the way you think about and deal with the challenges and obstacles in your life. It provides you with positive coping skills (and a technique for making those coping skills into habits) so that you are not only treating the problem currently at hand, but also giving yourself the strength and skills you need to prevent any problems from happening in the future.

Now that you have a broad understanding of how cognitive behavioral therapy works; what the process looks like; and what the ultimate goals of the methods are, you are ready to learn more about the specific cognitive behavioral therapy techniques and the four problems they are most effective at treating (namely, phobias, addictions, depression, and anxiety disorders).

Chapter 2: What Can You Treat with Cognitive Behavioral Therapy?

Cognitive behavioral therapy can be used to effectively treat a wide variety of different disorders. However, as mentioned in previous chapters, it has been proven the most effective at treating phobias, addictions, depression, and anxiety disorders.

In this chapter, you will get a brief overview of exactly what those four disorders involve. Afterward, you will learn about the major cognitive distortions that are at work in the negative thought processes contributing to these disorders. Finally, you will read briefly about the most effective cognitive behavioral therapy methods that you can use to treat them.

This chapter is not meant to be comprehensive. Instead, it is primarily intended to get you familiar with the terminology and technical terms that you are going to come across quite often in this book as well as in any other cognitive behavioral therapy resource that you use over the course of your treatment.

The 4 Disorders

- Phobias: phobias are extremely intense fears that go beyond any rational response to a threat. In some cases, the phobia is in response to something that is generally harmless (such as darkness, bathing, or noise). In other cases, the phobia is in response to something that is actually dangerous or harmful (such as drowning, burning, falling from a great height) but the fear is so exaggerated that it can cause more problems in a person's life than the actual threat itself.

  For example, if you are so afraid of drowning that you can't even drink water anymore, you run an extreme risk of dehydration. The causes of phobias can be complex and come from many sources.

You will learn more about them in chapter 4.

- Addiction: addiction is the mental or physical dependency (or, more often, a combination of both) on a particular substance, group of substances, or even habit. Many people have an addiction in some form or other. If you or anyone you know has talked about how difficult it is to wake up in the morning without a cup of coffee; that is an addiction. This can involve a physical addiction to the caffeine found in coffee but also a mental addiction to the whole ritual or routine of drinking coffee.

In some cases (such as the example above with coffee), it is not necessary to quit the substance cold turkey but simply to moderate how much you consume so that it does not pose a threat to your health. Coffee, to use the same example, can actually be great for your health if you only drink 1 or 2 cups per day. But if you find yourself drinking more than that, you may want to consider using cognitive behavioral therapy techniques to help you moderate your consumption.

For more serious substances such as hard drugs, alcohol, or tobacco; you will want to completely stop using the substance and break your addiction altogether. You will learn more about the mental and physical aspects of addiction in chapter 5 of this book. You will also learn more about the specific cognitive behavioral therapy methods that you can use to treat your addiction.

- Depression: depression as a disorder means much, much more than having a bad day or feeling sad after something traumatic has happened. In fact, feeling sad is not necessarily a negative thing. It is important to feel sad when bad things happen. This is how you learn to appreciate the good things in your life and a reminder to cherish your time on earth.

As a disorder, however, depression occurs when you become more or less permanently withdrawn from your life (or you experience long episodes of withdrawal). In most cases, nothing in particular is actually wrong (if you were to take a step back and look at your life from an objective standpoint) yet you still feel emotionally worn, listless, worthless, or even numb. Symptoms can be moderate to severe and it is extremely important to treat them, especially if you are suffering from suicidal thoughts. You will learn more about the specific symptoms of depression as well as the specialized cognitive behavioral therapy methods for treating them in chapter 6 of this book.

- Anxiety Disorders: anxiety comes in a wide variety of forms including generalized anxiety disorder, social anxiety disorder, obsessive compulsive disorder (OCD), and panic disorder. Anxiety disorders typically involve an exaggerated feeling of worry or panic in response to particular triggers. In this way, they are similar to phobias. However, phobias are highly specific (usually involving one type of trigger such as heights or small spaces).

Anxiety disorders, on the other hand, can include a variety of different triggers or, in some cases, a constant or extended feeling of anxiety in response to nothing in particular. Anxiety can be extremely debilitating to live with and, unfortunately, also extremely difficult to treat. Luckily, cognitive behavioral therapy has been proven as one of the most effective treatments for anxiety disorders and consistently has the best results for these cases. You will learn more about the causes and symptoms of anxiety disorders in chapter 7. You will also learn about the effective cognitive behavioral therapy methods that you can use to treat your anxiety.

Cognitive Distortions

Cognitive distortions are those errors in thinking that cause us to be unnecessarily negative or critical. We are all guilty of them to a certain extent but when they become deeply engrained habits, they can damage your ability to see any situation clearly.

- All or nothing thinking: this is when you see things in extremes or in black and white instead of noticing the shades of grey that are really there. This typically means only seeing the world in terms of complete positives or complete negatives. For example, in order to be successful, you might think that you have to achieve every single thing you have set out to do exactly as you plan to do it (or that you can't fail at anything you try). Such extreme thinking adds unnecessary pressure and causes you to feel like a total failure as soon as you encounter a challenge or obstacle.

- Over generalization: over generalization is the habit of assuming that one bad experience with a certain situation or person is proof that you will always only have bad experiences with that type of situation or person. For example, you might try to break out of your comfort zone and meet new people only to find that you meet rude or unfriendly people. If you over generalize, you will assume that any time you try to meet new people, it will be a bad experience (rather than realizing that it was just bad luck this time around and not all people are rude or unfriendly).

- Catastrophizing: this cognitive distortion happens whenever you take a certain negative situation and blow it way out of proportion. You immediately assume the absolute worst case scenario will happen as a result. For example, if you find a lump on your body, you might immediately assume it's a sign of cancer rather than any of a number of more common causes of lumps.

- Exaggerating: this is similar to catastrophizing in the sense that you blow something out of proportion. The difference is that this cognitive distortion is also associated with the behavior of overreacting. For example, if you ask someone for their opinion on something you wrote and they point out a few minor flaws or mistakes, you will become extremely upset and angry at the person.

- Ignoring the positives: this is an extremely common cognitive distortion. In fact, almost everyone does this to some degree. We tend to take the positive things in our lives for granted and only pay attention to the negative ones. This is usually because we falsely believe that we need to focus more on the negatives in order to fix them. However, it is equally important to focus on the positives in order to make sure that you can preserve them and don't let them slip away.

- Jumping to conclusions: this can be a dangerous cognitive distortion. It involves making a (usually negative) assumption without enough evidence. For example, if you ask a friend to hang out and they turn you down, you might jump to the conclusion that they no longer like you or are mad at you (rather than the more logical conclusion that they just don't have time at the moment)

- "Should" statements: these are usually statements referring to your personal standards you set for yourself (which are usually unrealistically high). They are statements that contain words like "should", "must", "never", or "always" even though such extreme words don't belong in the statement. It causes you to believe these personal standards are extremely rigid and inflexible. For example, you might say "I should never leave the house without makeup" even though there is actually no real negative risk for doing so (it is simply your own unrealistic personal standards of appearance and the false belief that others are holding you up to those same standards).

Cognitive Behavioral Therapy Methods

- Cognitive Processing Therapy: this variation of cognitive behavioral therapy is most often used in cases of posttraumatic stress disorder. The primary purpose is to help people process traumatic events and emotions in order to help people recover and reach a point of newfound strength. Although it is mostly used for PTSD cases, it is also helpful for those suffering from depression or anxiety who often get "stuck" on certain negative triggers or emotions.

- Exposure Therapy: exposure therapy has been proven highly effective in the treatment of phobias and anxiety disorders. This technique requires that the person face the source of their fear (or the triggers of their anxiety) in order to work on modifying their response to it. For example, someone with claustrophobia (fear of small spaces) might be required to stay in a small space for a certain length of time while practicing the positive coping skills they have learned through cognitive behavioral therapy. It can be very stressful at first but because it is done in a controlled and gradual way, it can help effectively eliminate the sense of fear or anxiety entirely.

- Acceptance and Commitment Therapy (ACT): this form of cognitive behavioral therapy focuses on mindfulness and other strategies for changing thoughts and behavior. It involves deep exploration of negative feelings and learning to accept rather than act on them. You also learn to face situations that may be negative or challenging rather than avoid them. This is a great technique for dealing with anxiety disorders. It can also be used for depression.

- Cognitive Therapy: this approach is exclusively focused on the cognitive aspects of cognitive behavioral therapy. That means you work entirely on changing your thought process and managing your emotional response (rather than working on changing behaviors). It is particularly helpful for depression as well as some anxiety disorders.

- Relaxation Training: relaxation training is very helpful in the treatment of all four of the disorders we will be looking at in this book but it is especially helpful for addiction and anxiety. It involves practicing relaxation techniques in order to relieve stress and manage stressful situations without becoming overwhelmed.

- Dialectical Behavior Therapy: whereas cognitive therapy focuses exclusively on changing your thought process, dialectical behavior therapy focuses exclusively on changing your behavior. It is designed to help eliminate or change negative behavior patterns (such as substance abuse or self harm). This makes it an extremely useful technique for the treatment of addiction and depression.

Chapter 3: Mental Health Assessment

In this chapter, you will learn how to conduct a mental health assessment on yourself so that you can start to better understand exactly what your problem is and where you should go from here.

Keep in mind that doing your own mental health assessment is not the same as having a professional do it. Do not use this as any kind of medical diagnosis. Even if your personal assessment shows that you have symptoms of depression or anxiety, avoid labeling yourself as "depressed" or someone with an anxiety disorder. Instead, use it as a tool for becoming more aware of yourself and for determining which of the cognitive behavioral therapy techniques will work the best in your situation.

To begin with, here is a list of the most recognizable symptoms of the four disorders this book is focusing on. Take a look at the lists of symptoms and note any of the ones that you have been experiencing.

Phobias

We tend to over-diagnose ourselves when it comes to phobias. Many people are afraid of spiders or clowns, for example, but few people have a debilitating fear of these things that prevents them from leading a normal, happy life. So when going through these symptoms (as well as the symptoms in the other 3 lists), keep in mind that in order to be a symptom, it has to actually be affecting your ability to live a happy, fulfilling life. For example, a fear of clowns becomes a phobia if that fear is preventing you from living out your dream of working at the circus.

First, we will look at the physical symptoms. These occur when the source of your fear is present:

- difficulty breathing
- racing heart

- chest pain
- shaking or trembling
- dizziness or feeling lightheaded
- upset stomach (or a churning feeling)
- hot flashes or cold flashes
- tingling sensations
- sweating

Now we will look at the emotional symptoms. These occur when the source of your fear is present but can also occur even when it is not there.

- overwhelming feeling of anxiety or panic
- an intense need to escape or get away
- dissociation (feeling detached from yourself or unreal)
- fear of losing control
- fear of losing your grasp on reality
- feeling like you will die (or lose consciousness)

- being aware that you are overreacting but feeling helpless to stop it or control your fear

Here are some additional signs that you have a phobia (and that you need to treat it as urgently as possible):

- the fear, anxiety, or panic is intensely disabling and prevents you from doing things you want to do
- awareness that your fear is unreasonable or exaggerated
- avoiding situations or places in order to avoid facing your phobia
- the phobia interferes with your normal routine or otherwise causes you unnecessary stress
- the phobia has lasted for at least 6 months

Addiction

As mentioned earlier, addiction can be both physical and mental (and often, it is both). Here are the physical symptoms of addiction:

- regular (usually daily) use of a substance (drugs, alcohol, cigarettes, etc)
- intense cravings for that substance that are difficult or impossible to ignore
- increasing tolerance for the substance (so that you need more and more of it to get the same effect).
- prolonged absence of the substance results in uncomfortable or painful symptoms (withdrawals) such as nausea, insomnia, sweating, restlessness, shaking, and so on.
- sudden weight loss or weight gain (or frequent fluctuations in your weight)
- changes in sleep pattern (or frequent fluctuations in your sleep pattern)

There are also psychological and behavioral symptoms of addiction:

- spending most of your time either using or thinking about the substance
- losing interest in or abandoning activities that you used to enjoy (sports, hobbies, going out with friends, etc)
- continuing to use the substance even though you know it's hurting you (or even though you would like to stop)
- having more fights with your loved ones or becoming withdrawn from the people you love
- putting yourself in dangerous or risky situations while under the influence or in order to get more of the substance
- neglecting your responsibilities
- unpredictable mood swings
- irritability
- anger management issues
- lack of motivation (lethargic, listless)
- anxiety or paranoia

It is also important to note that you can develop addictions to things aside from substances. Many people are addicted to gambling, shopping, or other activities that tend to provide an intense, short-term rush. The symptoms for these kinds of addictions can be very similar to the ones for substance addiction. You may even experience some of the same physical symptoms.

Depression

Here is a list of some of the common symptoms of depression:

- difficulty concentrating or focusing
- difficulty remembering details
- inability to make decisions
- fatigue or lack of energy
- feelings of shame, guilt or worthlessness
- feelings of hopelessness or helplessness
- insomnia or excessive sleeping
- irritability

- loss of interest in activities you once enjoyed
- lack of sex drive
- inability to feel pleasure or enjoyment from the things you once found pleasurable or enjoyable
- appetite loss or overeating
- chronic aches or pains
- headaches
- cramps or digestive problems that do not get better with treatment
- feelings of emptiness or detachment
- thoughts of suicide (or suicide attempts)
- engaging in risky behavior

Many of these symptoms can also occur temporarily in response to a traumatic event (such as the loss of a loved one, sudden unemployment, or other types of loss). In this case, while it is important to process the feelings (preferably using acceptance and commitment therapy); you should not confuse it as the sign of a chronic disorder.

Anxiety Disorders

Here are some of the common symptoms of anxiety disorders:

- feelings of panic, worry, fear, or uneasiness
- troubles sleeping
- cold or sweaty hands or feet
- shortness of breath
- heart palpitations
- restlessness or an inability to be calm
- dry mouth
- nausea
- dizziness
- muscle tension
- numbness or tingling of the hands or feet
- excessive stress or worry
- avoiding certain situations for fear that they may cause anxiety
- panic attacks

Next, you will learn about reconceptualization. That is, how to identify negative thoughts and the cognitive distortions that are at their roots. To do this, you'll need a pen and paper so that you can map out these negative thoughts.

First, identify a negative thought you have. It can be something like "I am overweight" or "I am not talented at any sports." Try to pick one that occurs often or that causes you the most distress. Write down that negative thought at the top of your page.

Next, think more carefully about why you believe this negative thing. What do you perceive as wrong or needing to be fixed? Using the overweight example again, you might think "If I weighed 20 pounds less, I would not be overweight" or "If I never ate sweets, I would not be overweight." Write down 1-3 statements like this.

Go back to chapter 2 of this book and look at the different kinds of cognitive distortions listed. For each statement you wrote in the previous step, identify which cognitive distortion it most closely resembles. For example, the statement "if I weighed 20 pounds less, I would not be overweight" is an example of all or nothing thinking because you believe that there is a precise weight you need to be at and anything above it is excess when in fact, your healthy weight will depend on a variety of factors and will be a weight range (like 130-160 pounds) rather than a single number.

Now, write down secondary thoughts or experiences that you use to confirm this original negative thought. For example, if you think you are overweight, you might write down "no longer fitting into my old jeans" or "not having sex with my partner as often as we used to." Write these below the original thought but leave some space between each for later.

In the space beneath each secondary thought, write down 1 or 2 possible alternative interpretations that do not confirm the original negative thought. For example, under "not having sex with my partner as often as we used to", you might write "we have both been more busy lately" or "I have felt too self-conscious to feel comfortable being naked."

You can follow this process for as many negative thoughts as you want. The more you do, the better because simply engaging in this process will help you gain perspective and practice challenging your negative thoughts.

Chapter 4: Cognitive Behavioral Treatments for Phobias

In chapter 3, you read about (and hopefully practiced) the first two phases of the cognitive behavioral therapy process. Namely: mental health assessment and reconceptualization. Now, it's time to begin with the third and fourth phases: skills acquisition and skills consolidation and application training.

Chapters 4 through 7 are focused on skills for treating specific disorders. You can either skip ahead to the chapter discussing the one that most closely relates to your own problem or you can read through all of them in order to gain a broader understanding of what skills and strategies are available for you to use.

If you choose to do the latter, you will be able to craft a more personalized cognitive behavioral treatment plan for yourself. This is because, while these strategies are considered most effective for certain disorders (such as exposure therapy for phobias), they can also be used to treat other problems. You can tweak or modify them to suit your purposes if you think they might be more effective.

With that in mind, this chapter will focus on cognitive behavioral therapy treatments for phobias.

Systematic Desensitization

This method is a great first step before taking the leap involved in exposure therapy. While exposure therapy requires you to face your fear in a real life situation (going to the top of a tall building or confining yourself to a small space), this method simply requires you to imagine or recall a situation in which you are facing your fear and then practice relaxation techniques to help diffuse and moderate the fear response.

This is best used as a first step prior to exposure therapy rather than a method all on its own. You will learn more about exposure therapy in the next section. To treat your phobia using systematic desensitization, complete the steps described below. To help explain the process a little better, we will be using the example of claustrophobia (a fear of small or confined spaces). To treat yourself, simply replace claustrophobia with your own phobia.

1. Learn and practice some relaxation techniques: cognitive behavioral therapy has developed a variety of useful and effective relaxation techniques. You will learn more about those in chapters 5 and 7 (which show how to use relaxation training to treat addiction and anxiety). You can use the techniques described in those chapters or another one that you have found on your own. The important thing is that you use a technique that you could potentially use if you were actually facing your phobia.

   For example, even if you find yoga relaxing, it may not be very practical to just start doing yoga in an elevator to counteract your claustrophobia. Deep breathing techniques or progressive muscle relaxation are two great options that you can realistically do in any situation. Once you have decided on one, practice it at home or anywhere where you feel safe just so that you can start to get the technique down and feel more confident in your ability to do it. You should continue practicing it on a regular basis because not only will you continue to improve your ability to relax yourself, the regular relaxation exercise will help to lower your base stress level so that you are more calm overall.

2. Build a fear hierarchy: for this step, you will need to write down a list of various situations related to your phobia that cause you varying degrees of fear or anxiety. These should be a combination of real experiences from your past and

situations that you have never actually been in but do still fear you might one day experience.

For example, a claustrophobic person might include something like "being in an elevator" which he or she has probably experienced at some point. He or she should also include something like "being in an elevator when it suddenly breaks down and I have to wait for rescue." This may never have happened but it is a situation that might cause anxiety to think about. Be as graphic and detailed as you can.

In that second example, you could expand on why the elevator broke down, who else is with you in it, how long you have to wait for help, or what resources you have with you. The details will help you vividly experience it in your imagination so that it feels more real. Altogether, your list of situations should be around 15 or so different situations. Make sure that they have differing levels of severity.

For example, you might have 5 situations that cause a low level of anxiety or fear, 5 that cause a medium level, and 5 that cause a high level of anxiety or fear. To keep them organized, you can write each situation on a separate index card (ranking their anxiety level on a scale of 1-10). Write the ranking on the back of the card so that you can't see it while reading the description of the situation.

3. Check the accuracy of your hierarchy: come back to your stack of index cards the next day and shuffle them. The anxiety level rank you assigned it should be on the back so that you can't see it. After thoroughly shuffling them, read each situation carefully and vividly imagine it. On a separate piece of paper, write down the rank you would give that situation. After you have done this for all 15 or so

situations, compare your new list with the rankings you assigned them yesterday. If it doesn't match up, make some adjustments until they are ranked in a way that feels honest and accurate.

4. Confront each situation in a relaxed state: after you have gotten your index cards organized and appropriately ranked by how much fear or anxiety the situation causes you, put them aside for a few days. In this time, continue practicing your relaxation technique that you chose in step 1. Once you feel comfortable with your ability to perform that technique, pull the cards out again but before looking at them, practice your relaxation technique until you feel calm and deeply relaxed.

Now, select the lowest ranked situation from your pile. Read the situation, close your eyes, and try to vividly imagine yourself in that situation. Imagine every minor detail (sights, sounds, smells, etc). The first time you do this, you should not overload yourself. If it starts to overwhelm you stop. But each session of systematic desensitization, try to increase the amount of time that you imagine yourself in this situation (until you can tolerate it for at least 30 seconds).

5. Stop and examine: after you have imagined yourself in the situation for as long as you can, rank the level of anxiety you feel (using the same 1-10 scale you used to rank the situations to begin with). Write this down. You should keep a notebook or journal dedicated to noting your anxiety levels so that you can track the progress of your desensitization sessions.

6. Relax: take about 1 minute to reestablish a sense of calm and relaxation.

7. Repeat: go through steps 4 through 6 again (focusing on the same situation). Repeat this process a few times. If you have gotten your anxiety level for a given situation down to 1, you can move on to the next one.

8. Relax: in each session, you should give yourself between 5-10 minutes to practice your relaxation technique so that you end the session in a state of calm. Think of it as your cool down after a rigorous work out.

Each of these desensitization sessions should last 30 minutes (with about 5-10 minutes at the beginning for establishing a state of relaxation and 5-10 minutes at the end to reestablish that state). While you do need to imagine the situations as vividly as possible, you do not want to expose yourself for longer than you can handle. Allow yourself to slowly build up tolerance for these situations.

Once you have gotten your anxiety level down to 1 for a given situation, move on to the next one. Always start each session with the last situation you imagined in your previous session.

To be effective, you need to fit at least 2 sessions in per week. This is the bare minimum. Ideally, you will do 5 sessions per week.

Exposure Therapy

Exposure therapy is a way of retraining your brain in the actual situation which causes you fear. In the above method, you are working on "desensitizing" yourself. That is, you are now able to imagine these fearful situations without feeling anxious or afraid. This is a major accomplishment.

The next step is to apply those same relaxation techniques to real life situations. The first you thing you need to know before doing exposure therapy is why it works:

In our brains, we have a part called the "amygdala." This part is responsible for the fight-or-flight response. It evolved to help us react instinctually to dangers (like predators, fires, or other deadly situations). Because of this, it learns through practice. If you have claustrophobia (to continue with the same example), it perhaps began with you having a negative experience in a small or confined space. That negative experience could be something severely traumatic or as simple as feeling a little uncomfortable. From that first situation, your amygdala already started to (incorrectly) learn that small spaces are negative or dangerous.

If after that you continued to avoid small spaces and each time you found yourself in one, you grew more and more uncomfortable, your amygdala would continue to intensify the fight-or-flight instinct in response to small spaces. That is, it increasingly starts to see small spaces as a danger that needs to be responded to in the same way that it once responded to the sight of a lion.

The thing is, the amygdala only activates and learns when you feel afraid. Therefore, the exposure therapy method works by retraining your brain in such a way that the amygdala no longer activates in response to your phobia.

When you first start using exposure therapy, it is going to be stressful. Ideally, you will do systematic desensitization (described above) first so that you will have already started to lower your fear response. To do exposure therapy, complete the following steps:

1. Find your phobia: go somewhere where the thing you fear is. If you are claustrophobic, this will be a small space. At the beginning, it is especially important that you have an exit route. As a claustrophobic, that means you should not start with an elevator. Instead, start with a closet or another small space where

you can get out if the process starts to overwhelm you.

2. Practice relaxation: before you confront your fear, practice your relaxation techniques (that you have been practicing since you began with desensitization) so that you are in a deep state of relaxation before the confrontation.

3. Acknowledge and accept: expose yourself to the fear, acknowledge the situation. That means paying attention to the sensations you feel and the situation around you. Don't try to ignore your fear or ignore the situation, face and acknowledge it. Tell yourself consciously exactly how you are feeling. Be detailed. Do not simply say "I am afraid." Instead say, "my heart is racing" or "my hands are shaking." Then, accept it. Don't feel bad or weak for feeling afraid right now. Tell yourself "It's ok that I am scared at this moment because this means that I am

bravely facing my fear rather than running away from it."

4. Practice relaxation: try to keep yourself from getting overwhelmed by practicing your relaxation techniques while you are confronting your fear. Continue the process of acknowledging and accepting while you do this.

5. Stop: when it gets to be too much and you can't endure it anymore, it's ok to leave the situation. The important thing is to try your best to leave calmly rather than panicked. Breathe deeply and walk at a normal pace, no matter how afraid you feel. Simply acting calm (even when you are terrified inside) will help start the process of retraining your amygdala to stop responding to your phobia as a dangerous threat.

You can repeat this process 2-3 times in one session if you feel you have the strength for it.

Try to fit in 2 or 3 sessions per week. But don't push yourself too far. Remember, you can always do another session but if you push yourself past your breaking point, the process will backfire. It's like beginning an exercise routine. If you want to build strength, you don't start with the amount of weight you want to be able to lift; you start with the amount you can lift right now. Start slow and build up your strength and relaxation skills.

Chapter 5: Cognitive Behavioral Treatments for Addiction

Addictions can be tough to handle on your own. While the cognitive behavioral therapy techniques described in this chapter can be highly effective; it is extremely advisable that you also get outside support to help keep you on track with your treatment and avoid relapse.

In this chapter, you will learn how to use relaxation training and dialectical behavior therapy in order to treat your addiction. For this chapter, we are going to use nicotine addiction as our example case.

Relaxation Training

Cognitive behavioral therapy has developed a variety of relaxation exercises that can help you overcome a variety of problems. They can even be used to treat everyday stress. In this chapter, we will focus on the exercises that tend to work best for addiction. In chapter 7, you will learn some additional relaxation exercises that are more targeted toward treating anxiety but could also be applied to addiction if you feel like they will be more effective for you. So make sure to read through both chapters.

1. Adopt an exercise routine: exercising might not sound like "relaxation" but it can actually have a powerful effect on your mind. Regular exercise has been proven to stabilize mood, reduce cravings (for addictive substances as well as food), and lower your stress levels. In many cases, your need to use a substance is triggered by an underlying problem (such as anxiety, depression, or even just a stressful life). Exercising regularly helps treat these underlying problems which helps eliminate the underlying causes of your addiction.

   In fact, studies have shown that just 10 minutes of fast-paced walking (particularly in natural settings) can completely eliminate your desire to smoke a cigarette. Choose any exercise routine that appeals to you. Many people find cardio exercise (like running or swimming) to be the most effective because these release dopamine and endorphins in your brain (the same exact chemicals that addictive substances release in your brain) and, therefore, offer a great alternative to your addiction that will still provide you with a kind of "high." To use exercise as a relaxation technique for addiction, you should try to get in at least 20 minutes of exercise per day. You can also use it as an emergency response to craving. That is, rather than restlessly struggle with your urge to light up a cigarette, go out for a run (or walk) instead.

2. Breathing exercises: this is a method of deep breathing combined with mindfulness. Take deep, slow breaths.

Allow your entire abdomen to expand as you inhale. Exhale slowly until your full breath has been released. While you are breathing, focus your mind. Count slowly to 10 as you inhale. When you reach 10, start back at 1 and count slowly to 10 as you exhale. Be aware of the sensations in your body. Feel the soles of your feet on the ground; feel the muscles on the top of your feet. Become aware of your entire body, working your way from the very bottom all the way up to the top of your head.

3. Progressive muscle relaxation: this method can be combined with the breathing exercises or done on its own. Lie down on your back somewhere comfortable. You start by tensing as many muscles as you possibly can. Then, beginning at the top of your head, start releasing the tension. With each exhalation, feel the muscles in your

forehead, cheeks, and chin release and come down.

Allow gravity to pull them deep into the bed (or couch, wherever you are laying down). Then, move down to your neck, your chest, your shoulders, and so on until you reach the tips of your toes. Remain in this state of complete release for about a minute. Then, tense your muscles again and repeat the process. Do this until a deep feeling of relaxation sets in.

Dialectical Behavior Therapy

Dialectical behavior therapy is a method of altering your harmful behaviors. It has been used effectively to treat suicidal people as well as many others with extremely severe problems. Many studies have come out showing that it is highly successful in the treatment of addiction.

The goals of dialectical behavior therapy are to help you better regulate your emotions; improve your ability to tolerate stress; increase mindfulness or self awareness; and build coping skills that help you deal with difficult people and situations without becoming overwhelmed. In this way, it targets the underlying causes of addiction. Because addictions often start as harmful coping mechanisms for trauma or stress; this therapy works to provide you with better, healthier coping skills to deal with trauma and stress so that the substance becomes unnecessary.

The process is broken into 4 stages. Rather than treating each stage like a separate step; approach them like bricks that you stack on top of each other. After you have focused on stage 1, continue to stage 2 while you still work on the skills you learned in stage 1.

1. Stage 1: this stage focuses on gaining control of your behavior. This includes the behavior of addiction (such as smoking

cigarettes) but also your behavior in other situations. To do this, you need to practice mindfulness (or self awareness). This means becoming aware of the present moment and what you are doing. It is for actions to become automatic, especially when you do them regularly. As a smoker, you often light up a cigarette without even thinking about the act. Instead, become aware of all the bodily sensations and exactly what you are doing. Pay attention to the act of removing the cigarette from the box; become aware of how it feels in your fingers. Roll it between your fingers and get a sense of its texture and consistency. Consider when the last time you had a cigarette was. Start regulating how often you smoke. Rather than try to completely quit all at once, decide to only smoke once every 3 or 4 hours. Gradually increase the amount of time between cigarettes on a weekly basis.

For example, the next week, leave 5-6 hours between cigarettes. Do this until you have gotten down to one cigarette per day (and then to no cigarettes). While you are smoking, do not let your mind drift to other topics, focus only on the smoke and the cigarette (this may sound a little boring but it's a good thing if smoking becomes boring). Practice the same awareness during all activities: washing the dishes, driving, drinking coffee, brushing your teeth. Try to be fully present in the moment throughout the day. It will be difficult at first (especially with the very routine things like brushing your teeth). But over time, you will improve and develop greater control over your behavior. It will also give you control over your cravings.

While 4 hours might seem like a long time (especially if you already crave another cigarette after 1 hour), it's easier to fight the craving if you know you only have to fight it for a couple more hours. Then, when you get better at resisting the craving for that short period of time, you will be able to increase the amount of time next week. When you get down to zero cigarettes, the cravings won't be entirely gone yet but your ability to resist your cravings will be much stronger than they were.

2. Stage 2: the second stage moves toward emotional experience. This means exploring your harmful or negative thoughts and processing past traumas and experiences. The ultimate goal is to reduce the pain and stress of these emotional experiences as well as reduce your feelings of guilt, denial, stigmatization, or other negative emotions associated with those experiences.

To do this, you will use a similar technique as you did in chapter 3 with reconceptualization. Get a pen and paper. Start with a single negative thought or past experience. Write that thought/experience down. Below it, draw a line down the center of the page to make 2 separate columns. On the left side, write down all of the emotions that are associated with that thought/experience. On the right side, write down the behaviors or actions that are associated with it. These include the behaviors/actions that trigger you to think about it and the behaviors/actions that result from you thinking about it. An example is provided for you at the end of this chapter.

3. Stage 3: in this stage, you work on improving your ability to solve everyday problems in a healthy and practical way. Rather than being overwhelmed by all these everyday stresses, you develop the skills to handle them without feeling the

need to escape. Begin by, learning to take one thing at a time and break things down into manageable steps. If you have a big task to accomplish, it can seem overwhelming and impossible if you just look at all of it as one big task. Instead, break it down into steps (and write those steps down).

For example, if you need to clean your entire house, it can seem overwhelming at first. So break it down into steps: kitchen, living room, bathroom, bedroom, etc. Then, break each of those down further. For the kitchen: wash dishes, clean counters, sweep, mop, etc. As you complete each step (focusing only on that step for the moment), what once seemed like an overwhelming task gets smaller and smaller.

You can apply this same logic to quitting your addiction. If you have a number of tasks to complete in a day (such as the smaller steps involved in cleaning your house), remember to take them one at a time. That is, while washing the dishes, don't start thinking about vacuuming the hallway. Focus on the dishes. If you encounter an everyday problem, rather than get overwhelmed with stress, examine the problem. What exactly is wrong? What might have caused it? What are some possible solutions? Which of those seems most practical? If there are no direct solutions to the problem, consider possible alternatives or compromises.

4. Stage 4: this final stage focuses on reinforcing the skills you have been working on in the previous 3 stages as well as cultivating a strong foundation of calm and joy. That is, even in the midst of the most stressful or upsetting situations, you will still be able to see the larger picture and remain happy overall (even if

you are a bit stressed and irritated at that particular moment).

For this, you will need to work on finding balance. The awareness you have been developing will help you do this. In any situation, clarify what you need; what you want; what you have to do; and how you feel. Practice negotiating between these things (because they will often conflict with each other) so that you find a balance between needs, wants, responsibilities, and emotions that works. This will mean prioritizing (needs come before wants, for example) so you won't always get exactly what you set out for in each category.

You may be obligated to do something that makes you unhappy (like needing to do the dishes even though you hate that chore) but you can strike a balance by deciding to get them out of the way (or if there are a lot of dishes, to do them in 20 minute sets and take breaks). The everyday problem solving skills you developed in stage 3 will help with this (as well as the emotional regulation skills from stage 2). As you learn to achieve this balance, you will no longer feel lacking in any area. You might have stressful days where the need to give yourself an emotional break becomes more important than the need to meet your obligations but all in all, you will be able to manage these different areas of your life in a harmonious way.

Thought/Experience:	
I dropped out of school when I was 16.	

Emotions/Feelings:	Behaviors/Actions:
• Shame • Guilt • Worthlessness • feeling stupid and unaccomplished	• Seeing my child struggle in school like I did • Getting frustrated when I encounter something I don't understand • Having a cigarette to escape the frustration

Chapter 6: Cognitive Behavioral Treatments for Depression

Of all the disorders that currently exist, depression has by far seen the most successful results from cognitive behavioral therapy. This form of treatment has actually proven to be as effective as taking antidepressant medication.

In this chapter, you will learn two strategies that have proven to be the most effective in the treatment of depression:

Cognitive Processing Therapy

1. Identify traumatic past experience(s): one major fact of depression is usually some form of traumatic experience in the past (whether it is abuse, a divorce, or another upsetting event). If you did not allow yourself (or otherwise did not have the opportunity) to process the pain and emotions at the time, then those are likely still plaguing you to this day. The first step

could take awhile for some people. And everyone is going to feel uncomfortable or afraid to dig these things back up. But you must act like the reckless explorer in uncharted waters, boldly following the current, wherever it takes you. Go deep into yourself and really see what is there. You can do this in the privacy of your own mind so you don't have to worry about others learning what is there without your permission.

2. Become aware of thoughts and feelings: once you have identified your traumatic experience(s). You need to explore them even further. What feelings come up to the surface as you think about them? There are two exercises you need to do for this step.

First, you need to write a detailed description of the experiences. Write every single thing you can remember. You don't have to show it to anyone. Just write it down. This act of writing it helps extract it from you, as if you were surgically slicing it out of yourself. You take the power from it. But it does not get the whole job done. The second exercise is to read that description again, add more details if you remember more. Then, on a new sheet of paper, write down what emotions come up for you now. What was the experience of reading it like for you on an emotional level?

3. Learn new coping skills: at this point, you are pretty raw and probably feeling as if you had been freshly cut open. Use the strategies you have learned in this book: relaxation training and the acceptance and commitment therapy method you will read about in chapter 7 will be particularly useful. This step should last the longest as retraining yourself to use new coping skills is a rigorous process that takes commitment and dedication.

4. Understand the changes in yourself: when the new coping skills start to feel a little more like habit take some time to do a follow up assessment. Read the description of the traumatic experience again. What feelings come up for you now? How is your emotional experience now different than it was before?

Cognitive Therapy

1. Track your negative thoughts: use the example at the end of this chapter to make your own thought record for your negative thoughts whenever you have a negative thought, briefly note it in your record. Try to make this a daily habit. Keep the record on your phone or in a notebook that you can carry with you so that it is easy to access.

2. Become aware of cognitive distortions: at the end of each day, note what sort of cognitive distortion(s) can be associated

with each negative thought you had throughout the day. Note this down next to the thought. Doing this regularly will help you to become more aware of your thoughts and what's really behind them.

3. Look for positives: after about 1 or 2 weeks of just repeating the first two steps on a daily basis, add this third step to your routine. After you have finished with your daily analysis of cognitive distortions, write down at least one positive thing about your day. It doesn't matter how small it might seem. The purpose of this exercise is to train your brain to start finding the positives in your day. They *are* there. Gradually increase the challenge by trying to add more and more positive things each day.

Chapter 7: Cognitive Behavioral Treatments for Anxiety

In this chapter, you will learn about two methods that have been shown to have the best results for anxiety disorders. You can use these strategies on their own or in combination with the other strategies you have read about in the previous chapters.

Relaxation Training

You have already learned some effective relaxation techniques in chapter five of this book (regarding addiction). You can also adapt those strategies to treat anxiety as well. Here are some additional relaxation techniques you can use:

- Yoga or Stretching: an exercise form like yoga or stretching which forces you to slow down and become aware of the sensations in your body is a great way to manage your anxiety. There are a number of reasons for this. First of all, it's slow paced but it can also be rigorous so that your overactive and anxious mind is still occupied with the activity rather than straying to other topics.

Secondly, it both slows and strengthens your heart while opening up your veins to improve circulation. All of this contributes to a decrease in the physical symptoms of anxiety which will make it much easier to manage the mental and emotional symptoms.

- Meditation: meditation is a great way to improve self awareness and concentration while decreasing stress. It will help strengthen your mind so that you are better armed against stressful situations. You can find many free guides to meditation online or buy a book, video, or other training course to help you learn how to do it.

Acceptance and Commitment Therapy

There are four major stages to Acceptance and Commitment Therapy (ACT) that make it well suited for helping you manage anxiety (as well as depression and even addiction).

- Awareness: the first step (which you might have noticed is similar to many first steps in the previous methods) is to improve self awareness. Pay attention to the links between thoughts, emotions, and behaviors. What thoughts contribute to your anxiety? What behaviors relate to your anxiety? How do these thoughts and behaviors make you feel?

- Acceptance: the next (and one of the hardest) steps is acceptance. Rather than blame yourself or feel ashamed that you have a problem with anxiety, learn to accept it. This doesn't mean continue to be anxious. Rather, accept that you are not perfect (and that *nobody* is). Accept the whole of your being (this includes your strengths as well, not just your weaknesses).

- Goal Setting: determine reasonable goals that you are passionate about. If you want to get further in your career, for example, figure out exactly how your anxiety is preventing you from doing that and come up with an actionable plan for overcoming your anxiety so that you can achieve your goals.

- Committed Action: in summary, this step asks you to just get to it! Once you have become more self aware and created a realistic plan for achieving your goals, the only thing left to do is get out there and start doing! Commit yourself to acting on your goals. Create daily tasks that you can manage to complete that will bring you closer to where you want to be and *who* you want to be.

Chapter 8: Final Tips and Advice

By this point, you already have all the information and strategies you need to get started with your own cognitive behavioral therapy treatment plan. Use the previous chapters to start constructing your own plan. In this chapter, you will read a few final tips to help you stay motivated and keep on track with your treatment plan.

- Always track your progress: this is important for a few reasons. First of all, it helps you see how you are doing with the treatment so that you can make adjustments along the way if you see that there is something which is not working. Secondly, tracking your progress helps make sure that keep us with your plan and don't skip any days. Sticking to a regular schedule with your treatment is an essential part of ensuring that it is successful.

Finally, tracking your progress gives you concrete and reliable ways to see how far you have come. In most cases, the difference from one session to the next is not going to be so dramatic that you can easily notice. Having a written record will help you see that you are, indeed, making progress.

- Have a support circle: when dealing with a severe disorder, it can be difficult to go on this journey alone. Identify the friends and family members you trust and keep them in the loop about what you are doing. If you don't have many people in your life that you can trust, find a support group. There are many out there for a variety of different issues. A support group can help you stay motivated throughout the process and even help you complete all of your sessions. Furthermore, they will likely be able to recognize progress in your problem before you do.

- Manage your goals: as mentioned earlier, you won't be miraculously cured after a session. You may not even notice significant changes in your first few sessions. You will first start to feel more raw and vulnerable before you start to feel stronger and more stable.

So if you set a goal for yourself to be totally cured in just one month, you are setting yourself up for disappointment. Set reasonable goals. The shortest time frame you can reasonably expect to make significant change is going to be about three months with intensive treatment or 6 months with less intensive treatment. Additionally, you should set some milestone goals along the road so that you stay on track and keep yourself motivated.

Warning Signs

Here are some warning sign that it may be necessary to seek professional help:

- Your addiction has reached a critical point and you are at serious risk of death.

- You have lost control over your addiction and isolated yourself from people who could help.

- Your phobia has become so severe as to prevent you from meeting your everyday needs and responsibilities.

- Your anxiety has become so severe as to prevent you from meeting your everyday needs and responsibilities.

- You have constant suicidal thoughts lasting for weeks.

- You are feeling suicidal and feel as if you have no personal support group to turn to.

Conclusion

Now that you have read through this book, you are ready to start putting together your own cognitive behavioral therapy treatment plan. Focus on the strategies that stood out to you most and remember to give yourself time to work through the 6 phases of the process (described in chapter 1 of this book). Do not rush through them with the hope of recovering as fast as possible.

Start with the mental health assessment (using the advice and guidelines described in chapter 3) and then move on to reconceptualization by identifying the negative thoughts that are contributing to your problem. Make sure to pay attention to the cognitive distortions that these negative thoughts are made up of. You should also work on finding positive thoughts that can replace (or at least counteract) these negative ones.

Once you have become skilled in reconceptualization, you can begin with your plan to learn and practice new, positive coping skills. This will be the most time consuming and challenging part of the process so give it plenty of time and remember to pay attention to the progress you are making (rather than just the progress you still need to make).

For additional help, there are a lot of free resources online that can offer you additional strategies and even guide you through the entire process. For example, you can try the MoodGYM which is a free online cognitive behavioral therapy training program specifically designed for the treatment of depression.

FearFighter is another great resource (although, not free unfortunately) that uses cognitive behavioral therapy techniques for the treatment of phobias and panic disorders. Another online service (also not free but still affordable) is Beating the Blues which focuses on treating depression and anxiety.

In addition to these online treatment programs, there are countless online resources for learning more about cognitive behavioral therapy techniques. There are also websites which offer free worksheets and treatment plan ideas for treating yourself with cognitive behavioral therapy. Simply doing a web search for "cognitive behavioral therapy" will bring up a long list of such resources.

With this book alone you can already start working on your own treatment. These online resources are just suggestions to provide you with additional support and to show you that there is nothing stopping you from making a change so that you can live a life of happiness and fulfillment.

Other books available by author on Kindle, paperback and audio

Self Confidence, Self Esteem And Self Love: How to Build Unbreakable Confidence through Self Love and by Raising Your Self Esteem